S0-BRI-572

WITHDRAWN. FOR FREE USE IN CITY
CULTURAL AND WELFARE INSTITUTIONS
MAY BE SOLD FOR THE BENEFIT OF
THE NEW YORK PUBLIC LIBRARY ONLY

New York's Industrial Growth

Robert Zillman and Henrietta M. Lily

Rosen
Classroom

New York

Published in 2012 by The Rosen Publishing Group, Inc.
29 East 21st Street, New York, NY 10010

Copyright © 2012 by The Rosen Publishing Group, Inc.

All rights reserved. No part of this book may be reproduced in any form without permission in writing from the publisher, except by a reviewer.

Book Design: Chris Brand

Photo Credits: Cover, p. 13 Library of Congress; p. 5 © Collection of New-York Historical Society; pp. 7, 15 (Clinton) © Hulton/Archive; p. 9 © Lee Snider; Lee Snider/Corbis; pp. 11, 15, 21 © Corbis; p. 13 (inset) © Library of Congress, Rare Books & Manuscripts; p. 17 © Rykoff Collection/Corbis; p. 17 (inset) © Independence National Historical Park; p. 19 © Schenectady Museum, Hall of Electrical History Foundation/Corbis; p. 19 (inset) Bettmann/Corbis

Library of Congress Cataloging-in-Publication Data
Zillman, Robert.
 New York's industrial growth/by Robert Zillman and Henrietta M. Lily.—1st ed.
    p. cm. — (Spotlight on New York)
  Includes index.
ISBN: 978-1-4488-5750-0 (lib. bdg.)
ISBN: 978-1-4488-5773-9 (pbk.)
6-pack ISBN: 978-1-4488-5774-6
1. Economic development—New York (State)—Juvenile literature. 2. Industrialization—New York (State)—History—Juvenile literature. 3. New York (State)—History—Juvenile literature. I. Lily, Henrietta M. II. Title. III. Series.

 HC107.N7Z55 2012
 338.9747—dc22

                                                            2011006919

Manufactured in the United States of America

Cover image: This picture of Brooklyn shows John Roebling's important creation, the Brooklyn Bridge. The bridge aided Brooklyn's growth in the late 19th century.

CPSIA Compliance Information: Batch #WS11RC: For Further Information contact Rosen Publishing, New York, New York at 1-800-237-9932

Contents

The Dutch in New York

The area that is now the state of New York has many **natural resources**. Long ago, **Native Americans** lived there, fishing, hunting, and growing crops. In the early 1600s, Dutch **merchants** arrived and began to **trade** there. The Dutch chose the area because they could get animal furs from Native Americans in return for metal tools, cloth, and weapons. The animal furs were worth large amounts of money in Europe.

The **region** also had other valuable natural resources, such as trees for **lumber**, good soil for farming, and **waterways** filled with fish. Waterways were also important for travel, building trading **ports**, and shipping **goods**. The trading region became a Dutch colony when the first **settlers** arrived in 1624. It was called New Netherland.

This map of the northeast coast of America was made around 1685 by Dutch mapmaker Nicolaes Visscher II. It is an improved copy of a map originally made around 1655. This map appeared in a book of maps that Visscher published around 1685.

The British in New York

The British took over New Netherland in 1664. It was renamed New York in honor of King Charles II's brother James, the duke of York. The settlers followed English **laws**. They paid **taxes** to England. England let **local governments** make some of their own laws.

Albany was the only **settlement** allowed to carry on the fur trade. New York City became the only port where all goods were loaded or unloaded. Towns were settled in the valleys of the Hudson and the Mohawk Rivers. Settlers built sawmills to turn trees into lumber. A hardworking settler could clear an **acre** of land in about ten days.

Agriculture was the most important business during the colonial period in New York. About 80 percent of New Yorkers made their living by farming.

7

New York Grows

By the early 1800s, people were coming from all over the world to live in New York. The **population** grew quickly. Farmers in the west sent their **produce** east to feed the people of New York City. Traders and merchants in the city sold the tools, furniture, and other goods farmers and settlers needed. The two groups built a strong trade.

This growth created new needs. New roads were built. Products had to be made in large numbers to meet the needs of the settlers. Businessmen such as Colonel Nathaniel Rochester did much to help New York grow. In the early 1800s, Colonel Rochester founded the town of Danville. It was built on the Genesee River. Soon, he built the village of Rochester. It grew around the **gristmills** he owned on the Genesee River. The town of Rochester became an **industrial center** in New York.

Philipsburg Manor in Tarrytown, New York, was established by Frederick Philipse in the 1700s. It was an important water-powered gristmill in New York before the American Revolution. Farmers once used gristmills to grind grain into flour.

Money in New York

During the late 1700s and early 1800s, British **manufacturers** chose New York City as a place to unload their goods. Thousands of merchants went to New York City to buy and sell goods from all over the world. New York came to control trade across the Atlantic Ocean, along America's East Coast, and with towns and cities that were further away from the coast. **Banks** were started to help manage the city's money.

On May 17, 1792, local businessmen created the first New York **stock market**. **Stocks** are a part of the **value** of a company. The men agreed to buy and sell the stocks of different companies. This became the New York Stock Exchange.

In 1794, a group of wealthy New Yorkers started the Bank of New York. By 1815, there were five banks in New York City. The banks were built in Manhattan on Wall Street and nearby. This picture shows how Wall Street looked around 1869. After 1840, the banking activities of the entire nation were centered in New York City. The smaller photo shows Wall Street today, with its famous statue of a charging bull.

Building Roads

New roads helped to connect farmers and the city, and to spread the wealth throughout New York State. Roads soon connected rivers and towns to major **trade routes**. New York's first roads were widened trails that had first been used by Native Americans. People drove horse-drawn carts and wagons over these rough dirt roads. Traveling was not easy. **Turnpikes** and **plank roads** were built to make travel faster and easier.

Between 1797 and 1807, 900 miles of turnpikes were built throughout New York State. By 1821, 278 turnpike companies had built 4,000 miles of roads in New York. Builders started making plank roads instead of turnpikes in the 1840s. The first plank road in New York was built north of Syracuse.

Pictured here is a page from a book of road maps published in 1789 by Christopher Colles. The small picture shows the cover of the book. Colles's book of maps was the first American road guide.

4

8

Buss

Attwood

Murray

Leggets

Powder
House
B

Cruger

A Survey
of the
Roads
of the
UNITED STATES
of
AMERICA
by Christopher Colles.
1789
REFERENCES.

Episcopal Church	Tavern	
Presbyterian Do.	Blacksmith Shop.	
Town House	Bridges mark'd by the	
Mill (for Grist & except otherwise mark'd	Road cutting the River	
	Gaol.	

Scale of one Mile.

C.Tiebout Sculp.

to Bloomingdale

to V.River

Tiebout

Mott

Mann

Baron Polnitz

Davenport

to North River

to Bayards

to Ferry

to Col White's

Watkins

10

Ellis

Adamsons

Van Zandt

Laury Hankenbroek

Gaine

hagen

Griersons

Neils

Delancy

9

Myers

13

Building the Erie Canal

New York **governor** De Witt Clinton wanted to make it easier and faster to **transport** goods. In 1817, he began work on the Erie Canal starting in Rome, New York. The **canal** was completed in 1825. It joined the Great Lakes to the Atlantic Ocean. It was 363 miles long, 40 feet wide, and four feet deep. The main canal had 83 **locks**.

The canal made transportation easier, faster, and less expensive. Trade with areas around the Great Lakes and beyond helped New York become a major **financial center**. Manufactured goods were shipped west to **pioneers** and western towns. Lumber and crops were shipped east to seaports. Before the canal was built, New York City was the **nation's** fifth-largest seaport. By 1840, it had become the nation's largest seaport.

The canal business made jobs for thousands of New Yorkers and greatly reduced shipping costs. For example, the canal lowered the cost of shipping goods between Buffalo and Albany from $100 per ton to under $10 per ton! This painting of the Erie Canal is a copy of one that was created by John William Hill in 1829.

De Witt Clinton

15

Railroads and Steam Systems

Inventions of the 1800s helped to grow **industry** in New York. Railroads could ship items faster and farther than any other kind of transportation. It became easier to send goods, such as meat that could spoil quickly, across the state.

Railroads helped **factories** grow more quickly. Large loads of **coal** could be sent to factories and businesses regularly. Coal was burned to heat water. This made steam, which was used to power machines. Machines could work faster and cheaper than humans could. This allowed the factories to produce more goods more quickly. By 1846, factories in Utica, New York, were using a **steam system** to run machines that made cloth. Soon, most factories used steam systems.

By 1860, railroads went to almost all parts of New York.

In 1807, an inventor named Robert Fulton created the first successful steam-powered boat, the *North River* (later called the *Clermont*). Shown here is the first New York steam-powered passenger train, the *De Witt Clinton*. This train first traveled from Albany to Schenectady on August 9, 1831.

Robert Fulton

Factories in New York

By 1860, there were factories all over New York State creating goods in large amounts. Cotton factories were built in Oneida *(oh-NYE-duh)*, Albany, Rensselaer *(ren-suh-LEER)*, and Dutchess counties. Gloversville and Johnstown became known for making gloves. Buffalo was home to the first **grain elevators**, which made storing and shipping grain faster and easier. Buffalo became the largest grain port in the world.

The Corning Flint Glass Works opened in Corning in 1868. In 1886, Thomas Edison set up Edison Machine Works in Schenectady *(skuh-NEK-tuh-dee)*. In 1892, this plant became the Edison General Electric Company. In 1888, George Eastman created the Kodak camera. In 1892, he started the Eastman Kodak Company in Rochester. All of these companies still exist today.

This is a 1904 photo of the General Electric plant. The Kodak advertisement is from 1900. The original Kodak camera came with a roll of film in it. After taking all 100 pictures, the owner sent the camera to the Eastman Kodak Company, where the film was processed. The photos and the camera (including new film) were then sent back to the owner.

Take a
KODAK
with you

The Kodak Girl

Life as a Factory Worker

Many factory workers lived and worked in unsafe conditions. Many of the machines were dangerous, and a small mistake could cause injury or death. Cities with factories were crowded. Workers lived in small apartments. Sometimes several families lived together in one room.

Children as young as eight years old worked 12 hours a day in hot, dirty factories. Thousands of children were sent to work in factories instead of going to school.

Some New York companies tried to help make things better. They thought worker health, safety, and happiness were important. In the early 1900s, Eastman Kodak put into place a system that allowed workers to earn more money if the company did well. The Endicott-Johnson Shoe Company of Johnson City and Endicott in central New York also gave its workers a **share** of the company's **profits**.

By 1860, half of New York City's population was made up of immigrants. Many of the immigrants had come to the United States looking for jobs. Hourly wages were low because immigrants needed work and were willing to take low-paying jobs. Slums—crowded areas where poverty and unhealthy living conditions are common—were filled with people who needed jobs. This photo from 1912 shows a slum on the Lower East Side of Manhattan.

Fighting for a Better Life

Many New Yorkers fought to improve life for workers in America. Many of them were **immigrants**. In 1886, a Jewish immigrant named Samuel Gompers organized the American Federation of Labor. It joined workers together to fight for better **wages** and safer **working conditions**. A woman named Fanny Wright was a member of the Workingmen's Party of New York City. She fought for workers' rights and free public schools for all children.

Leaders fought to **protect** children from having to work in factories. By the early 1900s, laws were passed that limited or outlawed child labor. **Labor unions** were formed to protect workers from unfair business owners. New laws protected workers from losing wages if an employer went out of business. These new laws improved working and living conditions for workers in New York City, New York State, and across the country.

Glossary

acre: Unit used to measure land.

banks: Places where people can save money and borrow money.

canal: A man-made waterway used for the travel of people or shipments of goods.

coal: A resource that can be burned to create energy.

factories: Places where goods are manufactured.

financial center: An important place for business and banking.

goods: Items that can be produced, bought, or sold.

governor: A person elected or appointed to manage a region.

grain elevators: Buildings for storing grain and sending it out.

gristmills: Mills for grinding grain.

immigrants: People who move to and settle in a place that is not their native land.

industrial center: An important city for manufacturing.

industry: Business of a specific type.

labor unions: Groups of workers who have banded together to fight for better working conditions.

laws: Rules of a state or country.

local government: The government of a town or city.

locks: Constructions for raising and lowering boats on canals.

lumber: Wood from cut trees.

manufacturers: People or groups who produce goods.

merchants: People who buy and sell goods.

nation: A group of people who share a common history, culture, and often, language.

Native Americans: The earliest peoples living in North America.

natural resources: Things produced by nature that can be used by people.

pioneers: The first people to settle in a new territory.

plank roads: Roads made of boards laid over dirt.

population: The number of people who live in a place.

ports: Places where water and land join, where people and merchandise can enter or leave by boat.

produce: Fresh fruits and vegetables.

profits: Money earned on top of the value of an item, from selling goods and services.

protect: To prevent from harm.

region: A large area of the Earth's land.

settlement: Established community where people live.

settlers: People who establish a place to live in a new land.

share: A part of a company given to its workers.

steam system: Machines run by the power of steam.

stock market: The market for buying and selling shares in companies.

stocks: Parts of a company that are sold to raise money.

taxes: Fees charged by the government on products, services, or activities.

trade: The business of exchanging goods for money or other goods.

trade routes: Pathways used to move goods to be traded.

transport: To move from one place to another.

turnpikes: Roads that people must pay to use.

value: How much something is worth.

wages: The amounts of money workers are paid.

waterways: Natural or man-made rivers and canals that can be used to transport goods.

working conditions: All the things that have to do with a worker's duties and workplace.

Index

Primary Source List

Cover. The City of Brooklyn lithograph. Currier & Ives, 1879.

Page 5. Engraved map of New Netherland. From a book of maps published around 1685 by Nicolaes Visscher II. Now in the New-York Historical Society.

Page 9. Philipsburg Manor. Established by Frederick Philipse in the early 1700s. Now a National Historic Landmark.

Page 11. *View of Wall Street from Corner of Broad.* Engraving from *Eighty Years' Progress of the United States,* published by L. Stebbins in 1869.

Page 13. Engraving from Christopher Colles's *A Survey of the Roads of the United States of America,* 1789.

Page 13 (inset). Title page. From Christopher Colles's *A Survey of the Roads of the United States of America,* 1789.

Page 15. *View of Erie Canal.* Copy of watercolor by John William Hill, 1829. Original now in New York Public Library.

Page 15 (inset). Portrait of De Witt Clinton. Engraving, ca. 1825. This portrait also appears on U.S. $1,000 bills issued in 1880.

Page 17. *De Witt Clinton* locomotive. The locomotive made its first run on August 9, 1831. A wheel from the locomotive is now in the Smithsonian Institution. The photograph shown here is undated.

Page 17 (inset). Portrait of Robert Fulton. Painted by Charles Willson Peale, 1807.

Page 19. Inside Building 15, General Electric's Schenectady Works. Photograph taken 1904. Now in the Schenectady Museum.

Page 19 (inset). Advertisement for Kodak camera. ca. 1900.

Page 21. Garment-making tenement, Elizabeth Street, Lower East Side, Manhattan. Photograph taken by Lewis Wickes Hine in March 1912.

Websites

Due to the changing nature of Internet links, The Rosen Publishing Group, Inc. has developed an online list of websites related to the subjects of this book. This site is updated regularly. Please use this link to access the list: **http://www.rcbmlinks.com/nysh/igny**